Favorite HYMNS *and* PRAYERS

Favorite Hymns and Prayers

PRINT: 978-08272-80489
EPUB: 978-08272-80496
EPDF: 978-08272-80502

CONTENTS

FAVORITE HYMNS

EASTER

CHRISTMAS

PATRIOTIC

COMMUNION

FAVORITE PRAYERS

Favorite HYMNS

2

Abide with Me

1. Abide with me; fast falls the eventide;
the darkness deepens, God, with me abide;
when other helpers fail, and comforts flee,
Help of the helpless, O abide with me.

2. Swift to its close ebbs out life's little day;
earth's joys grow dim; its glories pass away;
change and decay in all around I see;
O thou who changest not, abide with me.

3. I need thy presence every passing hour;
what but thy grace can foil the tempter's power?
Who like thyself my guide and stay can be?
Through cloud and sunshine, O abide with me.

4. I fear no foe, with thee at hand to bless;
ills have no weight, and tears no bitterness;
where is death's sting? Where, grave, thy victory?
I triumph still if thou abide with me.

5. Hold thou thy cross before my closing eyes;
shine through the gloom, and point me to the skies;
heaven's morning breaks, and earth's vain shadows flee;
in life, in death, O God, abide with me.

By Henry F. Lyte, 1847

All Hail the Power of Jesus' Name!

1. All hail the power of Jesus' name!
Let angels prostrate fall; bring forth the royal diadem,
and crown him Lord of all;
bring forth the royal diadem, and crown him Lord of all.

2. Ye seed of Israel's chosen race,
ye ransomed of the fall, hail him who saves you by his grace,
and crown him Lord of all;
hail him who saves you by his grace,
and crown him Lord of all.

3. O sinners, who can ne'er forget
the wormwood and the gall,
go spread your trophies at his feet,
and crown him Lord of all; go spread your trophies at his feet,
and crown him Lord of all.

4. Let every kindred, every tribe,
on this terrestrial ball, to him all majesty ascribe,
and crown him Lord of all;
to him all majesty ascribe, and crown him Lord of all.

5. O that with yonder sacred throng
we at his feet may fall!
We'll join the everlasting song, and crown him Lord of all;
we'll join the everlasting song,
and crown him Lord of all.

By Edward Perronet, 1779; alt. John Rippon, 1787

4

All the Way My Savior Leads Me

1. All the way my Savior leads me;
what have I to ask beside?
Can I doubt his tender mercy,
who through life has been my Guide?
Heavenly peace, divinest comfort,
here by faith in him to dwell!
For I know, whate'er befall me, Jesus doeth all things well;
For I know, whate'er befall me, Jesus doeth all things well.

2. All the way my Savior leads me,
cheers each winding path I tread,
gives me grace for every trial,
feeds me with the living bread.
Though my weary steps may falter,
and my soul athirst may be,
Gushing from the Rock before me, Lo! a spring of joy I see;
Gushing from the Rock before me, Lo! a spring of joy I see.

3. All the way my Savior leads me;
oh, the fullness of his love!
Perfect rest to me is promised
in my Father's house above.
When my spirit, clothed immortal,
wings its flight to realms of day,
This my song through endless ages: "Jesus led me all the way."
This my song through endless ages: "Jesus led me all the way."

By Fanny J. Crosby, 1875

Amazing Grace!

1. Amazing grace! How sweet the sound
that saved a wretch like me!
I once was lost, but now am found;
was blind, but now I see.

2. 'Twas grace that taught my heart to fear,
and grace my fears relieved;
how precious did that grace appear
the hour I first believed.

3. Through many dangers, toils, and snares,
I have already come;
'tis grace hath brought me safe thus far,
and grace will lead me home.

4. When we've been there ten thousand years,
bright shining as the sun,
we've no less days to sing God's praise
than when we'd first begun.

By John Newton, 1779; st. 4 anonymous

A Mighty Fortress Is Our God

1. A mighty fortress is our God, a bulwark never failing;
Our helper He, amid the flood of mortal ills prevailing:
For still our ancient foe doth seek to work us woe;
His craft and pow'r are great, and, armed with cruel hate,
On earth is not his equal.

2. Did we in our own strength confide,
our striving would be losing,
Were not the right Man on our side,
the Man of God's own choosing:
Dost ask who that may be? Christ Jesus, it is He;
Lord Sabaoth, His Name, from age to age the same,
And He must win the battle.

3. And though this world, with devils filled,
should threaten to undo us, We will not fear,
for God hath willed His truth to triumph through us;
The Prince of Darkness grim, we tremble not for him;
His rage we can endure, for lo, his doom is sure,
One little word shall fell him.

4. That word above all earthly pow'rs,
no thanks to them, abideth;
The Spirit and the gifts are ours
through Him Who with us sideth;
Let goods and kindred go, this mortal life also;
The body they may kill: God's truth abideth still,
His kingdom is forever.

By Martin Luther, 1529

Beneath the Cross of Jesus

1. Beneath the cross of Jesus I fain would take my stand,
the shadow of a mighty rock within a weary land;
a home within the wilderness, a rest upon the way,
from the burning of the noontide heat,
and the burden of the day.

2. Upon that cross of Jesus mine eye at times can see
the very dying form of one who suffered there for me;
and from my stricken heart with tears two wonders I confess:
the wonders of redeeming love and my unworthiness.

3. I take, O cross, thy shadow for my abiding place;
I ask no other sunshine than the sunshine of his face;
content to let the world go by, to know no gain nor loss,
my sinful self my only shame, my glory all the cross.

By Elizabeth C. Clephane, 1872

Blessed Assurance

1. Blessed assurance, Jesus is mine!
O what a foretaste of glory divine!
Heir of salvation, purchase of God,
born of his Spirit, washed in his blood.

2. Perfect submission, perfect delight,
visions of rapture now burst on my sight;
angels descending bring from above
echoes of mercy, whispers of love.

3. Perfect submission, all is at rest;
I in my Savior am happy and blest,
watching and waiting, looking above,
filled with his goodness, lost in his love.

Refrain
This is my story, this is my song,
praising my Savior all the day long;
this is my story, this is my song,
praising my Savior all the day long.

By Fanny J. Crosby, 1873

Blest Be the Tie That Binds

1. Blest be the tie that binds
our hearts in Christian love:
the fellowship of kindred minds
is like to that above.

2. When we are called to part,
it gives us inward pain;
but we shall still be joined in heart,
and hope to meet again.

By John Fawcett, 1872

10

Breathe on Me, Breath of God

1. Breathe on me, Breath of God,
fill me with life anew,
that I may love what thou dost love,
and do what thou wouldst do.

2. Breathe on me, Breath of God,
until my heart is pure,
until with thee I will one will
to do and to endure.

3. Breathe on me, Breath of God,
till I am wholly thine,
until this earthly part of me
glows with thy fire divine.

4. Breathe on me, Breath of God,
so shall I never die,
but live with thee the perfect life
of thine eternity.

By Edwin Hatch, 1878, alt.

Come, Ye Thankful People, Come

1. Come, ye thankful people, come,
raise the song of harvest home;
all is safely gathered in,
ere the winter storms begin;
God, our Maker, does provide
for our wants to be supplied;
come to God's own temple, come,
raise the song of harvest home.

2. All the blessings of the field,
all the stores the gardens yield,
all the fruits in full supply,
ripened 'neath the summer sky,
all that spring with bounteous hand
scatters o'er the smiling land,
all that liberal autumn pours
from its rich o'erflowing stores,

3. These to thee, our God, we owe,
source whence all our blessings flow;
and for these our souls shall raise
grateful vows and solemn praise.
Come, then, thankful people, come,
raise the song of harvest home;
come to God's own temple, come,
raise the song of harvest home.

By St. 1, Henry Alford, 1884; st. 2, 3, Anna Barbauld (18th century)

12

Fairest Lord Jesus

1. Fairest Lord Jesus,
ruler of all nature,
O thou of God to earth come down;
thee will I cherish,
thee will I honor,
thou, my soul's glory, joy, and crown.

2. Fair are the meadows,
fairer still the woodlands,
robed in the blooming garb of spring:
Jesus is fairer,
Jesus is purer,
who makes the woeful heart to sing.

3. Fair is the sunshine,
fairer still the moonlight,
and all the twinkling, starry hosts:
Jesus shines brighter,
Jesus shines purer,
than all the angels heaven can boast.

By Münster Gesangbuch, 1677; tr. Church Chorals and Choir Studies, 1850, alt.

Faith of Our Fathers

1. Faith of our fathers, living still
in spite of dungeon, fire and sword,
oh, how our hearts beat high with joy
whene'er we hear that glorious word!
Faith of our fathers, holy faith,
we will be true to thee till death.

2. The martyrs bound in prison chains
were still in heart and conscience free,
and bless'd would be their children's fate,
if they, like them, should live for thee!
Faith of the martyrs, holy faith,
we will be true to thee till death.

3. Faith of our mothers, we will love
both friend and foe in all our strife,
and preach thee, too, as love knows how,
by saving word and faithful life!
Faith of our mothers, holy faith,
we will be true to thee till death.

By Frederick W. Faber, 1849, alt.

God Be with You Till We Meet Again

1. God be with you till we meet again;
loving counsels guide, uphold you,
with a shepherd's care enfold you:
God be with you till we meet again.

Refrain:
Till we meet (Till we meet,) till we meet, (till we meet,)
till we meet at Jesus' feet; (till we meet;)
till we meet, (till we meet,) till we meet, (till we meet,)
God be with you till we meet again.

2. God be with you till we meet again;
unseen wings, protecting, hide you,
daily manna still provide you:
God be with you till we meet again.

3. God be with you till we meet again;
when life's perils thick confound you,
put unfailing arms around you:
God be with you till we meet again.

4. God be with you till we meet again;
keep love's banner floating o'er you,
smite death's threatening wave before you:
God be with you till we meet again.

By Jeremiah E. Rankin, 1880, alt.

God Will Take Care of You

1. Be not dismayed whate'er betide,
God will take care of you;
Beneath His wings of love abide,
God will take care of you.

Refrain:
God will take care of you,
Through every day, o'er all the way;
He will take care of you,
God will take care of you.

2. Through days of toil when heart doth fail,
God will take care of you;
When dangers fierce your path assail,
God will take care of you.

3. All you may need He will provide,
God will take care of you;
Nothing you ask will be denied,
God will take care of you.

4. No matter what may be the test,
God will take care of you;
Lean, weary one, upon His breast,
God will take care of you.

By Civilla D. Martin, 1904

Have Thine Own Way, Lord!

1. Have thine own way, Lord! Have thine own way!
Thou art the potter; I am the clay.
Mold me and make me after thy will,
while I am waiting, yielded and still.

2. Have thine own way, Lord! Have thine own way!
Search me and try me, Savior today!
Wash me just now, Lord, wash me just now,
as in thy presence humbly I bow.

3. Have thine own way, Lord! Have thine own way!
Wounded and weary, help me I pray!
Power, all power, surely is thine!
Touch me and heal me, Savior divine!

4. Have thine own way, Lord! Have thine own way!
Hold o'er my being absolute sway.
Fill with thy Spirit till all shall see
Christ only, always, living in me!

By Adelaide A. Pollard, 1902

He Leadeth Me: O Blessed Thought!

1. He leadeth me: O blessed thought!
O words with heavenly comfort fraught!
Whate'er I do, where'er I be,
still 'tis God's hand that leadeth me.

Refrain:
He leadeth me, he leadeth me,
by his own hand he leadeth me:
his faithful follower I would be,
for by his hand he leadeth me.

2. Lord, I would place my hand in thine,
nor ever murmur nor repine;
by waters still, o'er troubled sea,
still 'tis thy hand that leadeth me.

3. And when my task on earth is done,
when, by thy grace, the victory's won,
e'en death's cold wave I will not flee,
since God thro' Jordan leadeth me.

By Joseph H. Gilmore, 1862

18

Holy, Holy, Holy! Lord God Almighty!

1. Holy, holy, holy! Lord God Almighty!
Early in the morning our song shall rise to thee;
holy, holy, holy! Merciful and mighty,
God in three persons, blessed Trinity!

2. Holy, holy, holy! all the saints adore thee;
casting down their golden crowns around the glassy sea;
cherubim and seraphim falling down before thee,
God everliving, through eternity.

3. Holy, holy, holy! though the darkness hide thee,
though the sinful human eye thy glory may not see;
only thou art holy; there is none beside thee,
perfect in power, in love, and purity.

4. Holy, holy, holy! Lord God Almighty!
All thy works shall praise thy name in earth and sky and sea;
holy, holy, holy! Merciful and mighty;
God in three persons, blessed Trinity!

Descant:
4. Holy, God Almighty!
Thy works praise thee in earth and sky and sea;
God most holy, merciful and mighty!
God, all holy, blessed Trinity!

By Reginald Heber, 1826, alt.

How Firm a Foundation

1. How firm a foundation, ye saints of the Lord,
is laid for your faith in God's excellent word!
What more can be said than to you God has said,
to you who for refuge to Jesus have fled?

2. "Fear not, I am with thee, oh, be not dismayed,
for I am thy God, and will still give thee aid.
I'll strengthen thee, help thee, and cause thee to stand,
upheld by my righteous, omnipotent hand.

3. "When through the deep waters I call thee to go,
the rivers of woe shall not thee overflow;
for I will be near thee, thy troubles to bless,
and sanctify to thee thy deepest distress.

4. "When through fiery trials thy pathway shall lie,
my grace, all sufficient, shall be thy supply.
The flame shall not hurt thee; I only design
thy dross to consume, and thy gold to refine.

5. "The soul that on Jesus still leans for repose,
I will not, I will not desert to its foes;
that soul, though all hell should endeavor to shake,
I'll never, no never, no never forsake!"

By John Rippon's Selection of Hymns, 1787, alt.

I Am Thine, O Lord

1. I am thine, O Lord, I have heard thy voice,
and it told thy love to me;
but I long to rise in the arms of faith,
and be closer drawn to thee.

Refrain:
Draw me nearer, nearer, blessed Lord,
to the cross where thou hast died;
draw me nearer, nearer, nearer, blessed Lord,
to thy precious, bleeding side.

2. Consecrate me now to thy service, Lord,
by the pow'r of grace divine;
let my soul look up with a steadfast hope,
and my will be lost in thine.

3. O the pure delight of a single hour
that before thy throne I spend,
when I kneel in prayer, and with thee, my God,
I commune as friend with friend!

4. There are depths of love that I cannot know
till I cross the narrow sea;
there are heights of joy that I may not reach
till I rest in peace with thee.

By Fanny J. Crosby, 1875

I Love to Tell the Story

1. I love to tell the story
of unseen things above, of Jesus and his glory,
of Jesus and his love.
I love to tell the story, because I know 'tis true;
it satisfies my longings
as nothing else can do.

Refrain:
I love to tell the story,
'twill be my theme in glory, to tell the old, old story
of Jesus and his love.

2. I love to tell the story;
'tis pleasant to repeat
what seems, each time I tell it,
more wonderfully sweet.
I love to tell the story, for some have never heard
the message of salvation
from God's own holy word.

3. I love to tell the story,
for those who know it best
seem hungering and thirsting
to hear it like the rest.
And when, in scenes of glory, I sing the new, new song,
'twill be the old, old story
that I have loved so long.

By Katherine Hankey, c. 1868

22

I Need Thee Every Hour

1. I need thee every hour,
most gracious Lord;
no tender voice like thine
can peace afford.

Refrain:
I need thee, oh, I need thee;
every hour I need thee;
O bless me now, my Savior,
I come to thee.

2. I need thee every hour;
stay thou near by;
temptations lose their power
when thou art nigh.

3. I need thee every hour
in joy or pain;
come quickly, and abide
or life is vain.

4. I need thee every hour;
teach me thy will,
and thy rich promises
in me fulfill.

By Annie S. Hawks, 1872; refrain, Robert Lowry, 1872

It Is Well with My Soul

1. When peace, like a river, attendeth my way,
when sorrows like sea billows roll;
whatever my lot, thou hast taught me to say,
it is well, it is well with my soul.

Refrain:
It is well with my soul,
it is well, it is well with my soul.

2. Though Satan should buffet, though trials should come,
let this blest assurance control,
that Christ has regarded my helpless estate,
and hath shed his own blood for my soul.

3. My sin, oh, the bliss of this glorious thought!
My sin, not in part but the whole,
is nailed to the cross, and I bear it no more,
praise the Lord, praise the Lord, O my soul!

4. May God haste the day when my faith shall be sight,
the clouds be rolled back as a scroll;
the trump shall resound, and the Lord shall descend,
even so, it is well with my soul.

By Horatio G. Spafford, 1873

24

Jesus Is Tenderly Calling Thee Home

1. Jesus is tenderly calling thee home—
calling today, calling today;
why from the sunshine of love wilt thou roam,
farther and farther away?

Refrain:
Calling today, calling today;
Jesus is calling,
is tenderly calling today.

2. Jesus is calling the weary to rest—
calling today, calling today;
bring him thy burden and thou shalt be blest;
he will not turn thee away.

3. Jesus is waiting, O come to him now—
waiting today, waiting today;
come with thy sins, at his feet lowly bow,
come, and no longer delay.

4. Jesus is pleading, O list to his voice—
hear him today, hear him today;
they who believe on his name shall rejoice;
quickly arise and obey.

By Fanny J. Crosby, 1883

Jesus, Keep Me Near the Cross

1. Jesus, keep me near the cross:
there a precious fountain,
free to all, a healing stream,
flows from Calv'ry's mountain.

Refrain:
In the cross, in the cross,
be my glory ever,
till my raptured soul shall find
rest beyond the river.

2. Near the cross, a trembling soul,
love and mercy found me;
there the bright and morning star
sheds its beams around me.

3. Near the cross! O Lamb of God,
bring its scenes before me;
help me walk from day to day,
with its shadow o'er me.

By Fanny J. Crosby, 1869

Jesus Loves Me!

1. Jesus loves me! This I know,
for the Bible tells me so.
Little ones to him belong;
they are weak, but he is strong.

Refrain:
Yes, Jesus loves me! Yes, Jesus loves me!
Yes, Jesus loves me! The Bible tells me so.

2. Jesus loves me! This I know,
as he loved so long ago,
taking children on his knee,
saying, "Let them come to me."

3. Jesus loves me still today,
walking with me on my way,
wanting as a friend to give light
and love to all who live.

By St. 1, Anna B. Warner, 1860; st. 2, 3, David R. McGuire, c. 1970

Just a Closer Walk with Thee

1. I am weak, but thou art strong;
Jesus, keep me from all wrong;
I'll be satisfied as long
as I walk, let me walk close to thee.

Refrain:
Just a closer walk with thee,
grant it, Jesus, is my plea,
daily walking close to thee:
let it be, dear Lord, let it be.

2. Through this world of toil and snares,
if I falter, Lord, who cares?
Who with me my burden shares?
None but thee, dear Lord, none but thee.

3. When my feeble life is o'er,
time for me will be no more;
guide me gently, safely o'er
to thy shore, dear Lord, to thy shore.

WORDS: Anonymous

Just as I Am, Without One Plea

1. Just as I am, without one plea,
but that thy blood was shed for me,
and that thou bid'st me come to thee,
O Lamb of God, I come, I come!

2. Just as I am, though tossed about
with many a conflict, many a doubt;
fightings and fears within, without,
O Lamb of God, I come, I come!

3. Just as I am, thou wilt receive,
wilt welcome, pardon, cleanse, relieve;
because thy promise I believe,
O Lamb of God, I come, I come!

4. Just as I am, thy love unknown,
hast broken ev'ry barrier down;
now, to be thine, yea, thine alone,
O Lamb of God, I come, I come!

By Charlotte Elliott, 1835

Leaning on the Everlasting Arms

1. What a fellowship, what a joy divine,
leaning on the everlasting arms;
what a blessedness, what a peace is mine,
leaning on the everlasting arms.

Refrain:
Leaning, leaning,
safe and secure from all alarms;
leaning, leaning,
leaning on the everlasting arms.

2. O how sweet to walk in this pilgrim way,
leaning on the everlasting arms;
O how bright the path grows from day to day,
leaning on the everlasting arms.

3. What have I to dread, what have I to fear,
leaning on the everlasting arms?
I have blessed peace with my Lord so near,
leaning on the everlasting arms.

By Elisha A. Hoffman, 1887

Love Divine, All Loves Excelling

1. Love divine, all loves excelling,
joy of heaven, to earth come down;
fix in us thy humble dwelling,
all thy faithful mercies crown;
Jesus, thou art all compassion,
pure, unbounded love thou art;
visit us with thy salvation, enter every trembling heart.

2. Breathe, O breathe thy loving Spirit
into every troubled breast;
let us all in thee inherit, let us find thy promised rest;
take away our love of sinning; alpha and omega be;
end of faith, as its beginning, set our hearts at liberty.

3. Come, almighty to deliver,
let us all thy life receive;
suddenly return and never, nevermore thy temples leave.
Thee we would be always blessing,
serve thee as thy hosts above,
pray, and praise thee without ceasing,
glory in thy perfect love.

4. Finish, then, thy new creation; pure and spotless let us be,
let us see thy great salvation
perfectly restored in thee; changed from glory into glory,
till in heaven we take our place,
till we cast our crowns before thee,
lost in wonder, love, and praise.

By Charles Wesley, 1743

Marching to Zion

1. Come, we that love the Lord,
and let our joys be known;
join in a song with sweet accord,
join in a song with sweet accord
and thus surround the throne, and thus surround the throne.

Refrain:
We're marching to Zion, beautiful, beautiful Zion;
we're marching upward to Zion, the beautiful city of God.

2. Let those refuse to sing
who never knew our God;
but children of the heavenly King,
but children of the heavenly King
may speak their joys abroad, may speak their joys abroad.

3. The hill of Zion yields
a thousand sacred sweets
before we reach the heavenly fields,
before we reach the heavenly fields,
or walk the golden streets, or walk the golden streets.

4. Then let our songs abound,
and every tear be dry;
we're marching thru Emmanuel's ground,
we're marching thru Emmanuel's ground
to fairer worlds on high, to fairer worlds on high.

By Isaac Watts, 1707; refrain Robert Lowry, 1867

32

More Love to Thee, O Christ

1. More love to thee, O Christ,
more love to thee!
Hear thou the pray'r I make, on bended knee;
this is my earnest plea,
more love, O Christ, to thee,
more love to thee, more love to thee.

2. Once earthly joy I craved,
sought peace and rest;
now thee alone I seek, give what is best;
this all my pray'r shall be,
more love, O Christ, to thee,
more love to thee, more love to thee.

3. Let sorrow do its work,
send grief and pain;
sweet are thy messengers,
sweet their refrain,
when they can sing with me,
more love, O Christ, to thee,
more love to thee, more love to thee.

4. Then shall my latest breath
whisper thy praise; this be the parting cry
my heart shall raise,
this still its pray'r shall be,
more love, O Christ, to thee,
more love to thee, more love to thee.

By Elizabeth P. Prentiss, 1869

My Faith Looks Up to Thee

1. My faith looks up to thee,
thou Lamb of Calvary,
Savior divine!
Now hear me while I pray;
take all my guilt away;
oh, let me from this day
be wholly thine.

2. May thy rich grace impart
strength to my fainting heart,
my zeal inspire;
as thou hast died for me,
oh, may my love to thee
pure, warm, and changeless be,
a living fire.

3. While life's dark maze I tread,
and griefs around me spread,
be thou my guide;
bid darkness turn to day;
wipe sorrow's tears away;
nor let me ever stray
from thee aside.

By Ray Palmer, 1831, alt.

My Hope Is Built On Nothing Less

1. My hope is built on nothing less
than Jesus' blood and righteousness.
I dare not trust the sweetest frame,
but wholly lean on Jesus' name.

Refrain:
On Christ the solid rock I stand,
all other ground is sinking sand;
all other ground is sinking sand.

2. When darkness veils his lovely face,
I rest on his unchanging grace.
In every high and stormy gale,
my anchor holds within the veil.

3. His oath, his covenant, his blood
support me in the whelming flood.
When all around my soul gives way,
he then is all my hope and stay.

4. When he shall come with trumpet sound,
O may I then in him be found!
Dressed in his righteousness alone,
faultless to stand before the throne!

By Edward Mote, 1834

My Jesus, I Love Thee

1. My Jesus, I love thee, I know thou art mine;
for thee all the follies of sin I resign;
my gracious Redeemer, my Savior art thou;

Refrain:
if ever I loved thee, my Jesus, 'tis now.

2. I love thee, because thou hast first loved me,
and purchased my pardon on Calvary's tree;
I love thee for wearing the thorns on thy brow;

3. In mansions of glory and endless delight,
I'll ever adore thee in heaven so bright;
I'll sing with the glittering crown on my brow,

By William R. Featherstone, c. 1862

36

Near to the Heart of God

1. There is a place of quiet rest,
near to the heart of God;
a place where sin cannot molest,
near to the heart of God.

Refrain:
O Jesus, blest Redeemer,
sent from the heart of God,
hold us who wait before you
near to the heart of God.

2. There is a place of comfort sweet,
near to the heart of God;
a place where we our Savior meet,
near to the heart of God.

3. There is a place of full release,
near to the heart of God;
a place where all is joy and peace,
near to the heart of God.

By Cleland B. McAfee, 1903

Nearer, My God, to Thee

1. Nearer, my God, to thee, nearer to thee!
E'en though it be a cross
that raiseth me, still all my song shall be,
nearer, my God, to thee; nearer, my God, to thee,
nearer to thee!

2. When like the wanderer, the sun gone down,
darkness be over me, my rest a stone;
then in my dreams I'd be
nearer, my God, to thee;
nearer, my God, to thee, nearer to thee!

3. There let the way appear, steps unto heaven;
all that thou sendest me, in mercy given;
angels to beckon me
nearer, my God, to thee;
nearer, my God, to thee, nearer to thee!

4. Then, with my waking thoughts
bright with thy praise, out of my stony griefs
Bethel I'll raise; so by my woes to be
nearer, my God, to thee; nearer, my God, to thee,
nearer to thee!

5. Or if, on joyful wing
cleaving the sky, sun, moon, and stars forgot, upward I fly,
still all my song shall be, nearer, my God, to thee;
nearer, my God, to thee, nearer to thee!

By Sarah F. Adams, 1841

O, How I Love Jesus

1. There is a name I love to hear,
I love to sing its worth;
it sounds like music in my ear,
the sweetest name on earth.

Refrain:
O, how I love Jesus,
O, how I love Jesus,
O, how I love Jesus,
because he first loved me!

2. It tells me of a Savior's love,
who died to set me free;
it tells me of his precious blood,
the sinner's perfect plea.

3. It tells of one whose loving heart
can feel my deepest woe,
who in each sorrow bears a part,
that none can bear below.

By Frederick Whitfield, 1855; refrain anon.

O Master, Let Me Walk with Thee

1. O Master, let me walk with thee
in lowly paths of service free;
tell me thy secret; help me bear
the strain of toil, the fret of care.

2. Help me the slow of heart to move
by some clear, winning word of love;
teach me the wayward feet to stay,
and guide them in the homeward way.

3. Teach me thy patience; still with thee
in closer, dearer company,
in work that keeps faith sweet and strong,
in trust that triumphs over wrong.

4. In hope that sends a shining ray
far down the future's broadening way;
in peace that only thou canst give,
with thee, O Master, let me live.

By Washington Gladden, 1879

Open My Eyes, That I May See

1. Open my eyes, that I may see
glimpses of truth thou hast for me;
place in my hands the wonderful key
that shall unclasp and set me free.

Refrain:
Silently now I wait for thee,
ready, my God, thy will to see.
Open my eyes, illumine me, Spirit divine!

2. Open my ears, that I may hear
voices of truth thou sendest clear;
and while the wave-notes fall on my ear,
everything false will disappear.

3. Open my mouth, and let me bear
gladly the warm truth everywhere;
open my heart and let me prepare
love with thy children thus to share.

By Clara H. Scott, 1895

Praise God from Whom All Blessings Flow

Praise God from whom all blessings flow;
praise Christ, all creatures here below;
praise Holy Spirit evermore;
one God, triune, whom we adore.
Amen.

By Thomas Ken, 1674, alt.

42

Praise Him! Praise Him!

1. Praise him! praise him! Jesus, our blessed Redeemer!
Sing, O Earth, his wonderful love proclaim!
Hail him! hail him! highest archangels in glory;
strength and honor give to his holy name!
Like a shepherd Jesus will guard his children,
in his arms he carries them all day long:

Refrain:
Praise him! praise him! tell of his excellent greatness;
praise him! praise him ever in joyful song!

2. Praise him! praise him! Jesus, our blessed Redeemer!
For our sins he suffered, and bled and died;
he our Rock, our hope of eternal salvation,
hail him! hail him! Jesus the crucified.
Sound his praises! Jesus who bore our sorrows;
love unbounded, wonderful, deep and strong:

3. Praise him! praise him! Jesus, our blessed Redeemer!
Heavenly portals loud with hosannas ring!
Jesus, Savior, reigneth forever and ever;
crown him! crown him! Prophet and Priest and King!
Christ is coming! over the world victorious,
power and glory unto the Lord belong:

By Fanny J. Crosby, 1869

Rock of Ages, Cleft for Me

1. Rock of Ages, cleft for me,
let me hide myself in thee;
let the water and the blood,
from thy wounded side which flowed,
be of sin the double cure;
save from wrath and make me pure.

2. Not the labors of my hands
can fulfill thy law's demands;
could my zeal no respite know,
could my tears forever flow,
all for sin could not atone;
thou must save, and thou alone.

3. Nothing in my hand I bring,
simply to the cross I cling;
naked, come to thee for dress;
helpless, look to thee for grace;
foul, I to the fountain fly;
wash me, Savior, or I die.

4. While I draw this fleeting breath,
when mine eyes shall close in death,
when I soar to worlds unknown,
see thee on thy judgment throne,
Rock of Ages, cleft for me,
let me hide myself in thee.

By Augustus M. Toplady, 1776

44

Savior, Like a Shepherd Lead Us

1. Savior, like a shepherd lead us,
much we need thy tender care;
in thy pleasant pastures feed us,
for our use thy folds prepare.
Blessed Jesus, blessed Jesus,
thou hast bought us, thine we are;
blessed Jesus, blessed Jesus,
thou hast bought us, thine we are.

2. We are thine; do thou befriend us;
be the guardian of our way;
keep thy flock; from sin defend us;
seek us when we go astray.
Blessed Jesus, blessed Jesus,
hear thy children when we pray;
blessed Jesus, blessed Jesus,
hear thy children when we pray.

3. Early let us seek thy favor;
early let us do thy will;
blessed Lord and only Savior,
with thy love our spirits fill.
Blessed Jesus, blessed Jesus,
thou hast loved us, love us still;
blessed Jesus, blessed Jesus,
thou hast loved us, love us still.

By Dorothy A. Thrupp, 1836

Shall We Gather at the River

1. Shall we gather at the river,
where bright angel feet have trod,
with its crystal tide forever
flowing by the throne of God?

Refrain:
Yes, we'll gather at the river,
the beautiful, the beautiful river;
gather with the saints at the river
that flows by the throne of God.

2. On the margin of the river,
washing up its silver spray,
we will walk and worship ever,
all the happy golden day.

3. Ere we reach the shining river,
lay we every burden down;
grace our spirits will deliver,
and provide a robe and crown.

4. Soon we'll reach the shining river,
soon our pilgrimage will cease;
soon our happy hearts will quiver
with the melody of peace.

By Robert Lowry, 1864

Softly and Tenderly Jesus Is Calling

1. Softly and tenderly Jesus is calling,
calling for you and for me;
patient and loving, he's waiting and watching,
watching for you and for me.

Refrain:
Come home, come home,
ye who are weary, come home;
earnestly, tenderly, Jesus is calling—
calling, "O sinner, come home!"

2. Why should we linger when Jesus is pleading,
pleading for you and for me?
Why should we wait, then, and heed not his mercies,
mercies for you and for me?

3. O for the wonderful love he has promised,
promised for you and for me;
tho' we have sinned he has mercy and pardon,
pardon for you and for me.

By Will L. Thompson, 1880

Spirit of God, Descend upon My Heart

1. Spirit of God, descend upon my heart;
wean it from earth, through all its pulses move;
stoop to my weakness, mighty as thou art,
and make me love thee as I ought to love.

2. I ask no dream, no prophet ecstasies,
no sudden rending of the veil of clay,
no angel visitant, no opening skies,
but take the dimness of my soul away.

3. Teach me to feel that thou art always nigh;
teach me the struggles of the soul to bear:
to check the rising doubt, the rebel sigh;
teach me the patience of unanswered prayer.

4. Teach me to love thee as thine angels love,
one holy passion filling all my frame;
the baptism of the heavendescended Dove.
My heart an altar, and thy love the flame.

By George Croly, 1867

Standing on the Promises

1. Standing on the promises of Christ my king,
through eternal ages let his praises ring;
glory in the highest, I will shout and sing,
standing on the promises of God.

Refrain:
Standing, standing, standing on the promises of God my Savior;
standing, standing, I'm standing on the promises of God.

2. Standing on the promises that cannot fail,
when the howling storms of doubt and fear assail,
by the living Word of God I shall prevail,
standing on the promises of God.

3. Standing on the promises of Christ the Lord,
bound to him eternally by love's strong cord,
overcoming daily with the Spirit's sword,
standing on the promises of God.

4. Standing on the promises I cannot fall,
list'ning every moment to the Spirit's call,
resting in my Savior as my all in all,
standing on the promises of God.

By R. Kelso Carter, 1891

Sweet Hour of Prayer

1. Sweet hour of prayer! sweet hour of prayer!
that calls me from a world of care,
and bids me at my Father's throne
make all my wants and wishes known.
In seasons of distress and grief,
my soul has often found relief,
and oft escaped the tempter's snare
by thy return, sweet hour of prayer!

2. Sweet hour of prayer! sweet hour of prayer!
the joys I feel, the bliss I share
of those whose anxious spirits burn
with strong desires for thy return!
With such I hasten to the place
where God my Savior shows his face,
and gladly take my station there,
and wait for thee, sweet hour of prayer!

3. Sweet hour of prayer! sweet hour of prayer!
thy wings shall my petition bear
to him whose truth and faithfulness
engage the waiting soul to bless.
And since he bids me seek his face,
believe his word, and trust his grace,
I'll cast on him my every care,
and wait for thee, sweet hour of prayer!

By William Walford, 1845

Take My Life, and Let It Be

1. Take my life, and let it be
consecrated, Lord, to thee.
Take my moments and my days;
let them flow in ceaseless praise,
let them flow in ceaseless praise.

2. Take my hands, and let them move
at the impulse of thy love. Take my feet, and let them be
swift and beautiful for thee, swift and beautiful for thee.

3. Take my voice, and let me sing;
unto God my praise I bring. Take my lips and let them be
filled with messages from thee, filled with messages from thee.

4. Take my silver and my gold,
not a mite would I withhold; Take my intellect, and use
every power as thou shalt choose,
every power as thou shalt choose.

5. Take my will, and make it thine; it shall be no longer mine.
Take my heart, it is thine own;
it shall be thy royal throne, it shall be thy royal throne.

6. Take my love; my Lord, I pour
at thy feet its treasure store.
Take myself, and I will be
ever, only, all for thee, ever, only, all for thee.

By Frances R. Havergal, 1874

The Old Rugged Cross

1. On a hill far away
stood an old rugged cross,
the emblem of suffering and shame;
and I love that old cross
where the dearest and best
for a world of lost sinners was slain.

Refrain:
So I'll cherish the old rugged cross,
till my trophies at last I lay down;
I will cling to the old rugged cross,
and exchange it some day for a crown.

2. O that old rugged cross,
so despised by the world,
has a wondrous attraction for me; for the dear Lamb of God
left his glory above
to bear it to dark Calvary.

3. In that old rugged cross, stained with blood so divine,
a wondrous beauty I see, for 'twas on that old cross
Jesus suffered and died, to pardon and sanctify me.

4. To the old rugged cross
I will ever be true,
its shame and reproach gladly bear;
then he'll call me some day to my home far away,
where his glory forever I'll share.

By George Bennard, 1913

52

Trust and Obey

1. When we walk with the Lord
in the light of his word,
what a glory he sheds on our way!
While we do his good will,
he abides with us still, and with all who will trust and obey.

Refrain:
Trust and obey,
for there's no other way
to be happy in Jesus, but to trust and obey.

2. Not a burden we bear,
not a sorrow we share,
but our toil he will richly repay;
not a grief or a loss,
not a frown or a cross, but is blest if we trust and obey.

3. But we never can prove
the delights of his love
until all on the altar we lay;
for the favor he shows,
for the joy he bestows, are for them who will trust and obey.

4. Then in fellowship sweet
we will sit at his feet,
or we'll walk by his side in the way;
what he says we will do,
where he sends we will go; never fear, only trust and obey.

By John H. Sammis, 1887

We Gather Together

We gather together to ask the Lord's blessing;
Who chastens and hastens God's will to make known;
The wicked oppressing now cease from distressing;
Sing praises to God's Name; He forgets not his own.

Beside us to guide us, our God with us joining,
Ordaining, maintaining God's kingdom divine;
So from the beginning the fight we were winning;
Thou, Lord, were at our side, all glory be Thine!

We all do extol Thee, Thou Leader triumphant,
And pray that Thou still our Defender will be;
Let Thy congregation escape tribulation;
Thy Name be ever praised! O Lord, make us free!

WORDS: Anonymous/Unknown, 1597

54

We Have Heard the Joyful Sound

1. We have heard the joyful sound, Jesus saves, Jesus saves;
spread the gladness all a round, Jesus saves, Jesus saves;
bear the news to ev'ry land,
climb the steeps, and cross the waves,
onward, 'tis our Lord's command, Jesus saves, Jesus saves.

2. Waft it on the rolling tide, Jesus saves, Jesus saves;
tell to sinners, far and wide, Jesus saves, Jesus saves;
sing, ye islands of the sea,
echo back, ye ocean caves,
earth shall keep the jubilee, Jesus saves, Jesus saves.

3. Sing above the battle's strife, Jesus saves, Jesus saves;
by his death and endless life,
Jesus saves, Jesus saves;
sing it softly thro' the gloom,
when the heart for mercy craves,
sing in triumph o'er the tomb, Jesus saves, Jesus saves.

4. Give the winds a mighty voice, Jesus saves, Jesus saves;
let the nations now re joice, Jesus saves, Jesus saves;
shout salvation, full and free,
highest hills and deepest caves,
this our song of victory, Jesus saves, Jesus saves.

By Priscilla J. Owens, 1868

What a Friend We Have in Jesus

1. What a friend we have in Jesus,
all our sins and griefs to bear!
What a privilege to carry
everything to God in prayer!
Oh, what peace we often forfeit,
oh, what needless pain we bear,
all because we do not carry
everything to God in prayer.

2. Have we trials and temptations?
Is there trouble anywhere?
We should never be discouraged;
take it to the Lord in prayer!
Can we find a friend so faithful,
who will all our sorrows share?
Jesus knows our every weakness;
take it to the Lord in prayer!

3. Are we weak and heavy laden,
cumbered with a load of care?
Precious Savior, still our refuge,
take it to the Lord in prayer!
Do your friends despise, forsake you?
Take it to the Lord in prayer!
In his arms he'll take and shield you;
you will find a solace there.

By Joseph Scriven, 1855

56

When I Survey the Wondrous Cross

1. When I survey the wondrous cross
on which the Prince of glory died,
my richest gain I count but loss,
and pour contempt on all my pride.

2. Forbid it, Lord, that I should boast,
save in the death of Christ, my God;
all the vain things that charm me most
I sacrifice them to his blood.

3. See, from his head, his hands, his feet,
sorrow and love flow mingled down!
Did e′er such love and sorrow meet,
or thorns compose so rich a crown?

4. Were the whole realm of nature mine,
that were a present far too small;
love so amazing, so divine,
demands my soul, my life, my all.

By Isaac Watts, 1707

Where He Leads Me

1. I can hear my Savior calling,
I can hear my Savior calling,
I can hear my Savior calling,
"Take my cross and follow, follow me."

Refrain:
Where he leads me I will follow,
where he leads me I will follow,
where he leads me I will follow—
I'll go with him, with him all the way.

2. I'll go with him thru the judgment,
I'll go with him thru the judgment,
I'll go with him thru the judgment,
I'll go with him, with him all the way.

3. He will give me grace and glory,
he will give me grace and glory,
he will give me grace and glory,
and go with me, with me all the way.

By E. W. Blandy, 1890

Wonderful Words of Life

1. Sing them over again to me,
wonderful words of life;
let me more of their beauty see,
wonderful words of life.
Words of life and beauty,
teach me faith and duty;

Refrain:
beautiful words, wonderful words,
wonderful words of life,
beautiful words, wonderful words,
wonderful words of life.

2. Christ, the blessed one, gives to all,
wonderful words of life;
sinner, list to the loving call,
wonderful words of life.
All so freely given,
wooing us to heaven;

3. Sweetly echo the gospel call,
wonderful words of life;
offer pardon and peace to all,
wonderful words of life.
Jesus, only Savior,
sanctify forever;

By Philip P. Bliss, 1874

For EASTER

Alleluia! Sing to Jesus

Alleluia! Sing to Jesus; His the scepter, His the throne;
Alleluia! His the triumph, His the victory alone.
Hark! The songs of peaceful Zion
Thunder like a mighty flood: "Jesus out of every nation
Has redeemed us by His blood."

Alleluia! Not as orphans.Are we left in sorrow now;
Alleluia! He is near us:Faith believes, nor questions how.
Though the cloud from sight received Him
When the forty days were over, Shall our hearts forget His
promise: "I am with you ever-more"?

Alleluia! Bread of heaven, Here on earth our food, our stay;
Alleluia! Here the sinful. Flee to You from day to day.
Intercessor, Friend of sinners, Earth's Redeemer, hear our plea
Where the songs of all the sinless
Sweep across the crystal sea.

Alleluia! King eternal, Lord omnipotent we own;
Alleluia! Born of Mary, Earth Your foot-stool,
heaven Your throne. As within the veil You entered,
Robed in flesh, our great high priest,
Here on earth both priest and victim In the eucharistic feast.

Alleluia! Sing to Jesus; His the scepter, His the throne;
Alleluia! His the triumph, His the victory alone.
Hark! The songs of peaceful Zion. Thunder like a mighty flood:
"Jesus out of every nation Has redeemed us by His blood."

By William C. Dix, 1837-98

Christ Arose!

1. Low in the grave he lay, Jesus my Savior,
waiting the coming day, Jesus my Lord!

Refrain:
Up from the grave he arose,
with a mighty triumph o'er his foes;
he arose a victor from the dark domain,
and he lives forever, with his saints to reign.
He arose! He arose! Hallelujah! Christ arose!

2. Vainly they watch his bed, Jesus my Savior;
vainly they seal the dead, Jesus my Lord!

3. Death cannot keep its prey, Jesus my Savior;
he tore the bars away, Jesus my Lord!

By Robert Lowry, 1874

Christ the Lord Is Risen Today

1. Christ the Lord is risen today, Alleluia!
All creation, join to say, Alleluia!
Raise your joys and triumphs high, Alleluia!
Sing, O heavens, and earth reply, Alleluia!

2. Lives again our glorious King, Alleluia!
Where, O death, is now your sting? Alleluia!
Jesus died, our souls to save, Alleluia!
Where your victory, O grave? Alleluia!

3. Love's redeeming work is done, Alleluia!
Fought the fight, the battle won, Alleluia!
Death in vain forbids him rise, Alleluia!
Christ has opened paradise. Alleluia!

4. Soar we now where Christ has led, Alleluia!
Following our exalted Head, Alleluia!
Made like him, like him we rise, Alleluia!
Ours the cross, the grave, the skies, Alleluia!

By Charles Wesley, 1739, alt.

Crown Him with Many Crowns

1. Crown him with many crowns,
the Lamb upon his throne.
Hark! how the heavenly anthem
drowns all music but its own.
Awake, my soul, and sing
of him who died for thee,
and hail him as thy matchless King
through all eternity.

2. Crown him the Lord of life, who triumphed o'er the grave,
and rose victorious in the strife
for those he came to save; his glories now we sing
who died, and rose on high, who died, eternal life to bring,
and lives that death may die.

3. Crown him the Lord of peace,
whose power a scepter sways
from pole to pole, that wars may cease,
and all be prayer and praise.
His reign shall know no end, and round his pierced feet
fair flowers of paradise extend
their fragrance ever sweet.

4. Crown him the Lord of love;
behold his hands and side, those wounds, yet visible above,
in beauty glorified. All hail, Redeemer, hail!
For thou hast died for me; thy praise and glory shall not fail
throughout eternity.

By Matthew Bridges, 1851, and Godfrey Thring, 1874

64

In the Garden

1. I come to the garden alone,
while the dew is still on the roses;
and the voice I hear, falling on my ear,
the Son of God discloses.

Refrain:
And he walks with me, and he talks with me,
and he tells me I am his own,
and the joy we share, as we tarry there,
none other has ever known.

2. He speaks, and the sound of his voice
is so sweet the birds hush their singing,
and the melody that he gave to me
within my heart is ringing.

3. I'd stay in the garden with him
though the night around me be falling,
but he bids me go; through the voice of woe
his voice to me is calling.

By C. Austin Miles, 1913

O Sacred Head, Now Wounded

1. O sacred Head, now wounded, with grief and shame
weighed down,
Now scornfully surrounded with thorns, Thine only crown;
O sacred Head, what glory, what bliss till now was Thine!
Yet, though despised and gory, I joy to call Thee mine.

2. What Thou, my Lord, hast suffered, was all for sinners' gain;
Mine, mine was the transgression, but Thine the deadly pain.
Lo, here I fall, my Savior! 'Tis I deserve Thy place;
Look on me with Thy favor, vouchsafe to me Thy grace.

3. What language shall I borrow to thank Thee, dearest friend,
For this Thy dying sorrow, Thy pity without end?
O make me Thine forever, and should I fainting be,
Lord, let me never, never outlive my love to Thee.

4. Be Thou my consolation, my shield when I must die;
Remind me of Thy passion when my last hour draws nigh.
Mine eyes shall then behold Thee, upon Thy cross shall dwell,
My heart by faith enfolds Thee. Who dieth thus dies well.

Attributed by Bernard of Clairvaux, 1153
tr. by James W. Alexander, 1830

Were You There

Were you there when they crucified my Lord?
Were you there when they crucified my Lord?
Oh, sometimes it causes me to tremble, tremble, tremble.
Were you there when they crucified my Lord?

Were you there when they nailed him to the tree?
Were you there when they nailed him to the tree?
Oh, sometimes it causes me to tremble, tremble, tremble.
Were you there when they nailed him to the tree?

Were you there when they laid him in the tomb?
Were you there when they laid him in the tomb?
Oh, sometimes it causes me to tremble, tremble, tremble.
Were you there when they laid him in the tomb?

Were you there when God raised him from the tomb?
Were you there when God raised him from the tomb?
Oh, sometimes it causes me to tremble, tremble, tremble.
Were you there when God raised him from the tomb?

By Negro spiritual

for CHRISTMAS

68

Away in a Manger

1. Away in a manger, no crib for a bed,
the little Lord Jesus laid down his sweet head.
The stars in the sky looked down where he lay,
the little Lord Jesus, asleep on the hay.

2. The cattle are lowing, the baby awakes,
but little Lord Jesus, no crying he makes.
I love thee, Lord Jesus, look down from the sky,
and stay by my cradle till morning is nigh.

3. Be near me, Lord Jesus, I ask thee to stay
close by me forever, and love me, I pray.
Bless all the dear children in thy tender care,
and fit us for heaven to live with thee there.

WORDS: Anonymous (19th century)

Go Tell It on the Mountain

Refrain:
Go, tell it on the mountain,
over the hills and everywhere;
go, tell it on the mountain,
that Jesus Christ is born.

1. While shepherds kept their watching
o'er silent flocks by night,
behold throughout the heavens
there shone a holy light.

2. The shepherds feared and trembled,
when lo! above the earth,
rang out the angel chorus
that hailed the Savior's birth.

3. Down in a lowly manger
the humble Christ was born,
and God sent us salvation
that blessed Christmas morn.

WORDS: African-American spiritual; adapt. John W. Work, Jr., 1907

Hark! the Hearald Angels Sing

1. Hark! the herald angels sing,
"Glory to the newborn King;
peace on earth, and mercy mild,
God and sinners reconciled!"
Joyful, all ye nations, rise,
join the triumph of the skies;
with the angelic host proclaim, "Christ is born in Bethlehem!"
Hark! the herald angels sing, "Glory to the newborn King!"

2. Christ, by highest heaven adored;
Christ, the everlasting Lord!
Late in time behold him come, offspring of the Virgin's womb.
Veiled in flesh the Godhead see; hail the incarnate Deity,
pleased in flesh with us to dwell,
Jesus, our Emmanuel.
Hark! the herald angels sing, "Glory to the newborn King!"

3. Hail the heaven-born Prince of Peace!
Hail the Sun of Righteousness!
Light and life to all he brings,
risen with healing in his wings,
mild he lays his glory by,
born that we no more may die,
born to raise us from the earth,
born to give us second birth.
Hark! the herald angels sing, "Glory to the newborn King!"

By Charles Wesley, 1739, alt.

Joy to the World

1. Joy to the world, the Lord is come!
Let earth receive her King;
let every heart prepare him room,
and heaven and nature sing,
and heaven and nature sing,
and heaven, and heaven and nature sing.

2. Joy to the world, the Savior reigns!
Let all their songs employ;
while fields and floods, rocks, hills,
and plains repeat the sounding joy,
repeat the sounding joy,
repeat, repeat the sounding joy.

3. He rules the world with truth and grace,
and makes the nations prove
the glories of his righteousness,
and wonders of his love,
and wonders of his love,
and wonders, wonders of his love.

By Isaac Watts, 1719

O Come, All Ye Faithful

1. O come, all ye faithful, joyful, and triumphant,
O come ye, O come ye to Bethlehem;
come and behold him, born the King of angels;

Refrain:
O come, let us adore him, O come, let us adore him,
O come, let us adore him, Christ, the Lord!

2. Sing, choirs of angels, sing in exultation,
sing, all ye citizens of heaven above!
Glory to God, all glory in the highest;

3. Child, for us sinners poor and in the manger,
we would embrace thee, with love and awe;
who would not love thee, loving us so dearly?

4. Yea, Lord, we greet thee, born for our salvation,
Jesus, to thee be all glory given;
Word of the Father, now in flesh appearing;

Descant:
3, 4. O come, O come, let us adore him,
Christ, the Lord!

By John Francis Wade, 1743; tr. Frederick Oakeley, 1841, and others

O Little Town of Bethlehem

1 O little town of Bethlehem, how still we see thee lie!
Above thy deep and dreamless sleep
the silent stars go by.
Yet in thy dark streets shineth
the everlasting Light;
the hopes and fears of all the years are met in thee tonight.

2. For Christ is born of Mary, and gathered all above
while mortals sleep, the angels keep
their watch of wondering love.
O morning stars, together
proclaim the holy birth.
Your voices raise to God in praise; and peace to all on earth.

3. How silently, how silently
the wondrous gift is given!
So God imparts to human hearts
the joys of highest heaven.
No ear may hear Christ coming,
but in this world of sin,
where meek souls will receive him still,
the dear Christ enters in.

4. O holy Child of Bethlehem, descend to us, we pray;
cast out our sin, and enter in; be born in us today.
We hear the Christmas angels
the great glad tidings tell;
O come to us, abide with us, our God, Emmanuel.

By Phillips Brooks, 1868, alt.

Silent Night, Holy Night

1. Silent night, holy night,
all is calm, all is bright
round yon virgin mother and child,
holy infant so tender and mild,
sleep in heavenly peace,
sleep in heavenly peace.

2. Silent night, holy night,
shepherds quake at the sight,
glories stream from heaven afar,
heavenly hosts sing alleluia;
Christ, the Savior, is born!
Christ, the Savior, is born!

3. Silent night, holy night,
Son of God, love's pure light
radiant beams from thy holy face,
with the dawn of redeeming grace,
Jesus, Lord, at thy birth,
Jesus, Lord, at thy birth.

4. Silent night, holy night,
wondrous star, lend thy light;
with the angels let us sing,
alleluia to our King;
Christ, the Savior, is born,
Christ, the Savior, is born.

By Joseph Mohr, 1818; tr. John F. Young, 1863

The First Noel

1. The first Noel, the angel did say,
was to certain poor shepherds in fields as they lay;
in fields where they lay keeping their sheep,
on a cold winter's night that was so deep.

Refrain: Noel, Noel, Noel, Noel, born is the King of Israel.

2. They looked up and saw a star shining in the east,
beyond them far, and to the earth it gave great light,
and so it continued both day and night.

3. And by the light of that same star
three wise men came from country far;
to seek for a king was their intent,
and to follow the star wherever it went.

4. This star drew nigh to the northwest,
o'er Bethlehem it took its rest,
and there it did both stop and stay,
right over the place where Jesus lay.

5. Then entered in those wise men three,
full reverently upon their knee,
and offered there, in his presence,
their gold and myrrh and frankincense.

Descant: Noel, Noel, Noel, Noel, born is the King of Israel.

WORDS: Traditional English carol (17th century)

patriotic HYMNS

Mine Eyes Have Seen the Glory

1. Mine eyes have seen the glory of the coming of the Lord;
he is trampling out the vintage where the grapes of wrath are
    stored;
he has loosed the fateful lightning of his terrible swift sword;
his truth is marching on.

Refrain:
Glory, glory, hallelujah!
Glory, glory, hallelujah!
Glory, glory, hallelujah!
His truth is marching on.

2. He has sounded forth the trumpet that shall never call
    retreat;
he is sifting out all human hearts before his judgment seat;
O be swift, my soul, to answer him; be jubilant, my feet!
Our God is marching on.

3. In the beauty of the lilies Christ was born across the sea,
with a glory in his bosom that transfigures you and me;
as he died to make us holy, let us die to make all free,
while God is marching on.

By Julia Ward Howe, 1861, alt.

My Country, 'Tis of Thee

1. My country, 'tis of thee,
sweet land of liberty, of thee I sing;
land where my *fathers died,
land of the pilgrims' pride,
from every mountainside let freedom ring.

2. My native country, thee,
land of the noble free, thy name I love;
I love thy rocks and rills,
thy woods and templed hills;
my heart with rapture thrills like that above.

3. Let music swell the breeze,
and ring from all the trees
sweet freedom's song;
let mortal tongues awake,
let all that breathe partake,
let rocks their silence break, the sound prolong.

4. Our *fathers' God, to thee,
author of liberty, to thee we sing;
long may our land be bright
with freedom's holy light;
protect us by thy might, Great God, our King.

**Or* parents, parents'
By Samuel Francis Smith, 1831

O Beautiful for Spacious Skies

1. O beautiful for spacious skies,
for amber waves of grain,
for purple mountain majesties
above the fruited plain!
America! America! God shed full grace on thee,
and crown thy good with servanthood
from sea to shining sea.

2. O beautiful for heroes proved
in liberating strife,
who more than self their country loved,
and mercy more than life!
America! America! May God thy gold refine,
till all success be nobleness
and every gain divine.

3. O beautiful for patriot dream
that sees beyond the years
thine alabaster cities gleam,
undimmed by human tears!
America! America! God mend thine every flaw,
confirm thy soul in self-control,
thy liberty in law.

By Katherine Lee Bates, 1893

communion HYMNS

Break Thou the Bread of Life

1. Break thou the bread of life, dear Lord, to me,
as thou didst break the loaves beside the sea;
beyond the sacred page I seek thee,
Lord, my spirit pants for thee, O living Word.

2. Bless thou the truth, dear Lord, to me, to me,
as thou didst bless the bread by Galilee;
then shall all bondage cease, all fetters fall;
and I shall find my peace, my all in all.

3. O send thy Spirit, Lord, now unto me;
touch thou my longing eyes that I may see;
give me to eat and live with thee above;
teach me to love thy truth, for thou art love.

By St. 1, 2, Mary A. Lathbury, 1877; st. 3, Alexander Groves, 1913, alt.

Let Us Break Bread Together

1. Let us break bread together on our knees;
let us break bread together on our knees.

Refrain:
When I fall on my knees,
with my face to the rising sun,
O Lord, have mercy on me.

2. Let us drink wine together on our knees;
let us drink wine together on our knees.

3. Let us praise God together on our knees;
let us praise God together on our knees.

WORDS: African-American spiritual

The Church's One Foundation

1. The Church's one foundation is Jesus Christ her Lord;
she is his new creation, by water and the word:
from heaven he came and sought her to be his holy bride;
with his own blood he bought her, and for her life he died.

2. Elect from every nation, yet one o'er all the earth,
her charter of salvation, one Lord, one faith, one birth;
one holy Name she blesses, partakes one holy food,
and to one hope she presses, with every grace endued.

3. Though with a scornful wonder men see her sore oppressed,
by schisms rent asunder, by heresies distressed;
yet saints their watch are keeping,
their cry goes up, "How long?" and soon the night of weeping
shall be the morn of song.

4. Mid toil and tribulation, and tumult of her war
she waits the consummation of peace for evermore;
till with the vision glorious
her longing eyes are blessed, and the great Church victorious
shall be the Church at rest.

5. Yet she on earth hath union with God,
the Three in one, and mystic sweet communion
with those whose rest is won.
O happy ones and holy! Lord, give us grace that we
like them, the meek and lowly, on high may dwell with thee.

By Samuel J. Wesley

Favorite PRAYERS

Prayers for the Bread

Grant us, O God, the spirit, heart, and mind to be grateful, as we come in prayer to this communion table. Thank you for the food of this week and for this opportunity to partake of the spiritual bread in the name of Jesus. May we sense your presence, O God, in the breaking of bread and in our prayers of renewal and dedication. Guide us through the coming week. Amen.

O God, the giver of our daily bread, we pause to give you thanks. As we break the bread together, we ask that your presence might be felt here among us. In memory of Jesus we partake of his body, broken for us. Use us as your instruments of reconciliation and service throughout the days ahead. Amen.

Make us mindful, O Lord, of our debt to you for giving us daily bread for many days, weeks, and years. Renew us as we break together the communion bread of the Spirit. In the quiet of these moments, grant us a sense of renewed faith. We pledge ourselves to greater service in the coming days. Amen.

O Lord God, we give thanks that each day we receive food for the body. We pray that we may be more open to receive our needed bread of the Spirit. Bless the bread that we break here at the communion table. In this very act, O God, we remember Jesus and the assurance of eternal life. May your presence quicken our spirits so that your indwelling may be fruitful in our lives. Amen.

Most patient God, in thanksgiving we seek your presence as we break bread together at this communion hour. We remember Jesus and his infl uence in our lives. We ask that your Holy Spirit may fi ll us and direct us. Grant, O God, that we may fi nd renewal. Empower our commitment so that the days ahead may be lived in a way that is more pleasing in your sight. Amen.

— MORE Brief Prayers for Bread and Cup, by Russell F. Harrison

Prayers for the Cup

For the privilege of receiving this cup of blessing today, we give our thanks, O Lord. We come asking forgiveness for our many shortcomings and our sins. Help us to remember that Jesus died so that we might be forgiven and redeemed. Be present in our midst so that we might be guided by your Holy Spirit. Instill within us a new determination to live more fully the Christian way. Amen.

Creator of all people everywhere and in all time, we marvel at the mysteries of your creative power in human life. May this cup, in memory of Jesus, inspire us to better living in the days that lie ahead. Fill us with your Spirit so that we might become improved servants, seeking in company with millions everywhere to build your Kingdom here on earth. Amen.

O God of grace, bless this cup, which helps us to remember Jesus and the manner in which his life was given for each one of us. May your Spirit empower us to overcome our blindness and our weakness so that we might be of greater service to your Kingdom. In humility, and yet in confidence, we pray for your continuing guidance. Amen.

God of time and eternity, we are grateful for this communion hour. May partaking of the cup prepare us spiritually for the task of being Christian in our daily relationships. Help us, O God, to see more clearly your mission for us in the world today. With your help we can bring a better world into being. Amen.

Ever-present God, as we drink the cup, may it be a cup of thanksgiving for your love, which surrounds us and sustains us. By remembering Jesus, may our own confession of faith become a renewal of our commitment. Make us more effective instruments of your love, so that we might make this world a better place and may touch with good those persons who are around us. Amen.

— *MORE Brief Prayers for Bread and Cup, by Russell F. Harrison*

Psalm 23

The LORD is my shepherd, I shall not want.
    He makes me lie down in green pastures;
he leads me beside still waters; he restores my soul.
He leads me in right paths for his name's sake.

Even though I walk through the darkest valley, I fear no evil;
for you are with me; your rod and your staff—
    they comfort me.

You prepare a table before me in the presence of my enemies;
you anoint my head with oil; my cup overflows.
Surely goodness and mercy shall follow me
    all the days of my life,
and I shall dwell in the house of the Lord my whole life long.

The Lord's Prayer

Our Father in heaven, hallowed be your Name,
your Kingdom come,
your will be done
on earth as in heaven.
Give us today our daily bread.
Forgive us our sins (debts/trespasses)
as we forgive those who sin against us (our debtors/
those who trespass against us).
Save us from the time of trial,
and deliver us from evil.
For the kingdom, the power,
and the glory are yours, now and forever. Amen.

Serenity Prayer

Lord, grant me the serenity
To accept the things I cannot change,
The courage to change the things I can,
And the wisdom to know the difference.
Living one day at a time,
Enjoying one moment at a time
Accepting hardship as the path to peace.
Taking, as He did,
This sinful world as it is, not as I would have it:
Trusting that He will make all things right
If I surrender to His will.
That I may be reasonably happy in this life,
And supremely happy
With Him forever in the next.

— *Reinhold Niebuhr*

Psalm 19 (King James Version)

1The heavens declare the glory of God; and the firmament
sheweth his handywork.

2Day unto day uttereth speech, and night unto night sheweth
knowledge.

3There is no speech nor language, where their voice is not
heard.

4Their line is gone out through all the earth, and their words
to the end of the world. In them hath he set a tabernacle for
the sun,

5Which is as a bridegroom coming out of his chamber, and
rejoiceth as a strong man to run a race.

6His going forth is from the end of the heaven, and his circuit
unto the ends of it: and there is nothing hid from the heat
thereof.

7The law of the LORD is perfect, converting the soul: the
testimony of the LORD is sure, making wise the simple.

8The statutes of the LORD are right, rejoicing the heart: the
commandment of the LORD is pure, enlightening the eyes.

9The fear of the LORD is clean, enduring for ever: the
judgments of the LORD are true and righteous altogether.

10More to be desired are they than gold, yea, than much fine
gold: sweeter also than honey and the honeycomb.

11Moreover by them is thy servant warned: and in keeping of
them there is great reward.

12Who can understand his errors? cleanse thou me from secret faults.

13Keep back thy servant also from presumptuous sins; let them not have dominion over me: then shall I be upright, and I shall be innocent from the great transgression.

14Let the words of my mouth, and the meditation of my heart, be acceptable in thy sight, O LORD, my strength, and my redeemer.

Jesus Prayer

Lord Jesus Christ, Son of God, have mercy on me, a sinner.

Cleanse the Thoughts of Our Hearts

Almighty God, unto whom all hearts are open, all desires known, and from whom no secrets are hid, cleanse the thoughts of our hearts by the inspiration or your Holy Spirit, that we may perfectly love you, and worthily magnify your holy Name.

— *Gregorian Sacamentary (6th century), alt.*

O Lord, Support Us

O Lord, support us all the day long, until the shadows lengthen and the evening comes, and the busy world is hushed, and the fever of life is over, and our work is done.
Then, Lord, in your memory grant us safe lodging, and a holy rest, and peace at the last; through Jesus Christ our Lord.

—*Attributed to John Henry Newman, England, 19th-century British churchman*